THE
THORN
KEY
FAIRY TALES IN VERSE

JEANA JORGENSEN

Poems that have been previously published are listed here, with gratitude for the editors who selected them for their first print appearance, and are reprinted with permission:

"Woven of Silence & Thistles" – *Stone Telling*, 2016

"King Wivern" – *Mirror Dance*, 2017

"Worth the Wait" – *Enchanted Conversation*, 2017

"Seasick" – *Strange Horizons*, 2017

"Secrets" – *Liminality*, 2017

"The Witch's House" – *Liminality*, 2018

"Blunt Weapon" and "Daughter of Daedalus" – *Wyrd & Wyse*, 2018

"Daddy Death" – *Glittership*, 2018

"Walking on Knives" – *The Future Fire*, 2019

"What Happened to the 12th Dancing Princess" – *Liminality*, 2019

"Tenacity" and "Selkie" – *Quatrain.fish*, 2020

"The Twelve Brothers" – *Nevermore*, 2021

"Swan Maiden," "Fairies' Gifts," and "Half-Life of a Mermaid" – *3 Moon Magazine*, 2021

"Excerpts from Hans Christian Andersen's 'The Little Mermaid'" – *Crow & Cross Keys*, 2021

"Betrothed to a King," "The Ogre's Heart," "Given or Sold or Stolen Away," "Coat of a Thousand Furs," and "The Old King Dreams" – *Lothlorien Poetry*, 2021

"The Sleeper Awakened" – *Enchanted Conversation*, 2021

"Rapunzel's Mother(s)" and "You Can't Just Leave Your Car These Days" – *Patchwork Folklore Journal*, 2021

"Snow White Goes Gray" – *Crow & Cross Keys*, 2022

"Bluebeard" – *The Orange & Bee*, 2024

CONTENTS

ALSO BY JEANA JORGENSEN

Folklore 101: An Accessible Introduction to Folklore Studies

Fairy Tales 101: An Accessible Introduction to Fairy Tales

Sex Education 101: Approachable Essays on Folklore, Culture, &

History

FOREWORD

It sounds cliché, but I've always loved poetry, both reading it and writing it. I started going to open mic nights in high school despite being extremely shy and introverted, and so I had experience sharing my work early on. I've published poems in various outlets for over ten years, but only recently had the idea to publish my fairy-tale-themed poetry in a collection.

Some of these poems have been previously published, in a range of magazines and journals, some online and some in print. Others have encountered few sets of eyes, or none except mine. All of these poems revolve around fairy tales, sometimes questioning what counts as a "happily ever after" and sometimes offering alternatives. I wanted to gather them all into one place so that they could be easily read together instead of sending readers on quests to try to find all of them; save your questing for the mundane world.

I've included a list of content or trigger warnings below, since some of these poems explore the violent underside of fairy tales and of human experience more generally. Not that they needed much of a nudge to go there; many fairy tales already contain death, dismemberment, the threat of incest and cannibalism, and so on. There is a whole history of fairy tales before Disney arrived on the scene, and while fairy tales do contain many magical moments and wishes granted, they are ultimately shaped by human hands and human needs, including the need to survive the splintering of a family, the betrayal of a loved one, and much, much worse.

At the end of the book is an afterword putting some of these poems into conversation with scholarship on fairy tales as well as with my life. Reading it is entirely optional; I like to think that the poems speak for themselves, but I offer it to the curious. And there are proverbs aplenty about the uses and abuses of curiosity.

I leave this thorn key in your hands. Careful, it bites. What will you use it to unlock?

LIST OF CONTENT WARNINGS/TRIGGERS

Abuse: "Beauty & the Beast in Berkeley," "Donkeyskin," "Rapunzel's Mother(s)," "Trafficked," "What Happened to the 12th Dancing Princess," "The Witch's House," "Woven of Silence and Thistles"

Animal death: "Coat of a Thousand Furs"

Break-up/relationship-ending/divorce: "Half-Life of a Mermaid," "King Wivern," "The Ogre's Heart," "Rapunzel's Mother(s)," "The Witch's House," "Woven of Silence and Thistles"

Incest: "Coat of Many Furs," "Donkeyskin," "Donkeyskin Does the Dishes," "The Old King Dreams"

Homophobia: "Daddy Death," "Rapunzel's Mother(s)," "What Happened to the 12th Dancing Princess"

Pregnancy: "Rapunzel's Mother(s)"

Substance use: "Rapunzel's Mother(s)," "What Happened to the 12th Dancing Princess"

Door of Red and White Roses

GIVEN OR SOLD OR STOLEN AWAY

Wife of white bear,

Captive of beast,

Wyvern's bride,

Monster's feast:

Here is a list of women,

Girls like you and me

Promised to exotic husbands

Never to be set free.

Fathers who gamble

And brothers who lie

Trolls who cheat

And mothers who die:

Who to blame

When we're stolen away,

Who to curse

On our wedding day?

Give me just one story

And make it true,

Of a girl who escaped,

Who grew wings and flew.

Or better yet, was never sold,

Never given, never stolen away,

Who was her own story's hero,

Not a man's stowaway.

Betrothed to a King

I knew what I was getting into,

wedding a king who'd been

betrothed before.

Princesses vanish all the time:

turned into frogs and cats,

made housekeeper to a witch,

buried in holes.

These things happen.

Our alliance was a good one,

my family noble enough,

the king kind enough,

the staff pleasant,

the mother-in-law overjoyed.

The courtship slipped by

like a sunset

and the rumors were mercifully few

(the first bride could charm birds from the sky,

toss flour onto coals to make exquisite bread,

dance like a gazelle, and of course she was beautiful).

I allowed myself one small rebellion

against tradition.

I thought I was safe.

Lulled into security by her absence,

by his slow, small smiles,

by fleeting touches that became lingering,

I ignored my upbringing.

(A marriage is just an alliance;

a good wife's first duty is to bear children,

and next, to be a virgin on her wedding night,

and finally, to love her husband.)

The night before the wedding,

I crept unseen to his chambers.

I spelled one guard to sleep;

What good is magic if unused?

Hesitant at first, his caresses transformed

From dove kisses to dog bites,

Firm and insistent, binding us together.

I did not regret it til the next day,

Sitting at the wedding feast,

Sharing wine and sly glances.

Suddenly a girl—

Radiantly beautiful, haggardly thin.

Her smile a knife to my heart,

His eyes a blow to my soul.

My mind stuttered on a spell

(Iron shoes? Cavern exile?

Transform into a bird,

Chain to a sea monster?)

And too late I heard his voice

Ringing out into the stunned silence.

"If I lost the key to a treasure coffer

And had a new one made,

But the old key was found,

Which should I keep?"

A key.

I was a key.

An object to be used

And discarded.

My fingers,

Wrapped around my wedding wine,

Stiffened and tensed,

Clutched as if for her throat.

There was little left for me to do

But disappear, my wedding dress

Clinging like a shroud

With my cheeks afire:

Anger, betrayal, shame.

No longer a token for my family,

Shunted from the traffic in women

To...what? Where? Who would I become?

Would I wear these wintry colors

To hide a trampled heart,

The hot flush of shame, forever?

This much I know:

There is no safety in life.

Never count on a princess to stay gone.

And I am no key.

THE OGRE'S HEART

I know the secret

of the ogre's heart

within the casket.

I am throwing my clothes

into garbage bags

and bundling those into my car

and wiping snow from my hair

while the white silent world

vibrates with the sound of my breathing.

I will get through this.

There is a trunk within my storage unit

with a hollow ottoman inside it

and wrapped in a blanket is

our wedding album.

Inside the album

Inside the blanket

Inside the ottoman

Inside the trunk

Is...not my heart, but a memory of it:

sun-filled laughter,

gleaming eyes and smiles,

transparent images,

ghost-selves of a dead past.

In the fairy tales,

the princess held captive by the ogre

betrays him with the location of his heart,

given to the hero on a bed of promises:

eager, yielding, spreading thighs/lips/heart.

Outside the storage unit

frost cakes on my face

and, shivering, I unload the last of it,

the last vestiges of this life

failed, this union unfulfilled.

Frozen, I see the remainder stored:

tax forms, cutlery, the fucking welcome mat.

Mechanically, I move it all inside.

The ogre is not the villain.

The ogre stored his heart in a casket

to protect it, not from some dumb ass hero

but from the unfiltered humanity around him,

that could so effortlessly reduce him to tears.

The ogre has important ogre shit to do.

The ogre has to get on with his day.

The ogre cannot afford to be distracted

by weeping princesses, sniveling heroes, and the like.

If I had tears to weep,

they would freeze on my cheeks.

But no heart means no tears.

Blank-faced, I'm only aware

of an uncomfortable fullness when I blink.

The last of it is stored.

I'm leaving my home.

The secret of the ogre's heart

(in a casket, inside a duck, inside a swan)

glitters within my eyes.

Nobody will unlock it or find it

until I'm ready to stop my mad pacing,

panting, my frenetic plotting to escape

the prison that looks like a house.

The stories tell of the princess running away.

Maybe she was, but I know the truth:

the ogre had run away long

before the princess ever showed up.

The ogre is still running.

It's easier to run when you are heartless.

Someday, if some stupid hero doesn't destroy it first,

the ogre will tenderly lift his heart from the casket

and reinsert it into his chest,

take a deep, shuddering breath

and begin to live once more.

I lock my storage unit.

I drive away.

My heart is not inside,

it is nowhere to be found.

I gracefully extricate myself

(to whispers of, "how does she hold it together?")

And I survive mostly-whole.

And the only reason I smile

is because of my heart,

locked safely away,

shut away so that I can do the unthinkable

and endure the extremes of human emotion

and maybe someday adopt a princess

who will show me why storing hearts in places

is not the best way to live forever.

SELKIES

Before there was ghosting, there were selkies:

Sleek swimmers who carved through water,

Carved a place inside a heart and home,

Then re-skinned themselves, glinting away from the shore.

SECRETS

Monsters have a different ratio of

captivity time to trust

than the rest of us.

They collect treasure, it's true,

but also secrets, and those unspilled words

weigh heavier on ridged spines

and massive bone structures

than you'd think.

By the time the princess oh-so-coyly

asked the ogre how he could be harmed,

the secret was poised to fly from his lips,

ready to be free at last.

I wonder if the ogre knew what he'd done:

if he regretted the sharing,

if he shuddered to remember

the sticky intimacy of letting someone in like that.

I learned that I don't like it.

After we fucked in your San Francisco shoebox

you asked me to tell you a story,

and without thinking

I gave you the key to my soul.

(I'm not retelling the story here,

do you think I'm stupid?)

Point is, I gave you a piece of me

that was far more intimate than the sex

and I didn't even realize I'd done it

until it was too late.

And now I can't stop thinking about

giants and ghouls and all the rest

who told these girls they'd captured

about their hearts hidden in chests,

the hairs that, when pulled, kill them.

I wonder if they knew what they were doing

when they spoke the truth

that would become their doom.

Did they wish the words would clamber

back into their lips, unsaid?

Leaving them more time with a sullen princess

to pick lice from their misshapen heads?

Or were these beasts ready to go:

had they seeded the tea-time chatter

with hints of their demise,

dropped in casually like

lemon rind into muffin batter?

Knowing that you know this about me

makes me feel like the skin's been stripped away

and I am naked, vulnerable, defenseless.

So of course I ghosted you.

I mean, not entirely;

I'm not a monster.

Half-Life of a Mermaid

You can only tolerate the glassy look in her eyes,

Failing to understand human meaning,

For so long before you start leaving hints.

You know that old, oiled cloth?

I've heard some folks store theirs in a coat closet.

Honey, doesn't this Netflix documentary about fish migration patterns

Look fascinating? Worth a watch? Honey?

You ask if she would like you to rehang the curtains;

In the pause that follows, you can tell

She is translating your airborne words into clicks in her mind.

You leave more desperate hints:

Maps to the beach where you found her,

X marking the spot where you first saw her emerge from the spraying waves,

And where you flung a flannel on her ice-cold shoulders.

"Wouldn't a vacation be nice?" you say, and

She nods blankly, her damp ringlets bobbing

(Her hair is always wet, and your wood floors

Have needed extra care ever since you brought her home).

You leave the fish-leather skin around:

A doorstop one week, a tablecloth another.

When you host brunch, guests are disturbed at the "smelly coat."

You cease hosting brunch.

After a particularly difficult week—

Salt crusting every surface in the house,

Ruining two antique tables—

You bundle her up and drive her to the coast.

Her nostrils flare like gills as you approach the shore,

Waving the scaled skin in front of her,

Flagging a path among the rocks and sand.

"You can stop pretending for me," you say, voice breaking.

"Your home is here, I know it now."

Her hair glistens in the rising sun as she stares over the sea,

And when you drape the skin over her shoulders

It melts into her hair, dribbling down her body

Until her tail emerges where legs once were

With a thump, taking her down to the sand.

She mouths your name—

"Laura"—

Before the waves roll over her.

She does not look back.

You do not wave.

BEAUTY & THE BEAST IN BERKELEY

I've always hated roses:

sickeningly sweet smells

nostril-climbing,

sense-dulling,

sleep-walking me around town

arm-in-arm with you, smiling

the whole time.

They lined up my father's debts with my FAFSA

and there was no way for me to attend,

let alone live in Berkeley.

Oh but that one scholarship—

Dad signed me away

(it included free housing).

Who could say no

to the gothic mansion

in the Berkeley hills?

Though it came with the stipulation

that I must always smile,

that we would go on daily walks,

that my rent included

tending the roses.

The smile wore my face

like a mask of flesh;

the smile opened its lips

to drink lattes from ceramic bowls

at that French café on Shattuck

and it was only when one shard

pricked my thumb like a thorn

and the coffee catapulted into my lap

that I woke up, horrified,

shedding my skin mask,

remembering there was a me before,

knowing I had to leave you.

Stinking of roses,

I completed my degree

in

three

years.

I didn't always hate roses

until you trapped me with them,

kept me to your home

enchanted my mind into slumber

while telling me

it was love.

What Happened to the 12th Dancing Princess

(Circa 1946)

You won me, went to war, returned and wanted your wife back:

wanted to fill my nights with the press of your body

and fill our home with your medals and your presence.

But while you were gone I filled my own nights:

from factory to dance hall I danced with no man,

would not begin again, not after twirling midnights in women's arms

til our shoes were tattered—and I wasn't about to start now.

You put a stop to it the only way you knew how

but the seed would not take in my body worn thin

by wartime rations and sleepless evenings dancing.

Shouts, stares, and locks couldn't keep me from spinning

when they were imposed by you, but an errant wife

who's a deviant, well...lock her up before Valium was

a gleam in its maker's eye and see if they'll give her lithium

here or electroshock therapy there, make her behave

like a woman should, better a shorn head and straitjacket

than a wife who strays, won't obey.

No more nights of dancing: replaced by fever dreams

of descent underground, silver branches scratching me

as I flee, my mangled feet carrying me toward

my beloved who dances without me across water,

on tiles of gold and ash, but I can never reach her,

can never cross: the soupy fog clutches me

tight, the medicine holds me here between our worlds

and maybe someday girls like me can dance their shoes

to pieces on floors that don't pierce them with wedding rings and
pills—

the girls you made sure I'll never know, they will know me:

I will die here but my canvas-clad body will be one pair

of worn out shoes that propel lithe feet forward,

forward in time, always toward each other,

until we can clasp hands once again:

those soft and strong hands reaching for me,

waiting, my dancing loves.

HEDGEHOG

Hedgehog-boy,

curled up tight—

what wish or curse

gave you such spines?

Was it being shunned,

kicked, tormented,

lied to, degraded?

Or did you tell yourself

you were always unwanted,

unlovable, too sharp?

I see you

curl in

to protect

your soft belly

(defensive, pokey,

licking wounds

when you think

no one is looking).

And I'll wait

but I only ask:

please don't direct

those spines at me,

don't assume I'm like

the girls with lips of lies

who would use you

and use up any love

to get what they want.

When you press sharpness

to my throat,

I'll wait,

exhale,

knowing sure as

the cock's crow

at dawn

you'll see me

for me

eventually.

King Wivern

(or, an old Danish fairy tale with a happy ending)

King Wivern said to his bride:

"Fair maiden, shed a shift!"

And his bride replied:

"Husband, shed a skin!"

Oh we were an unlikely match

But our romance blossomed

And for a time

We brought out the best in each other.

Shed a skin; shed a shift

I compromised this; you gave up that.

Neither of us was happy.

The king had been married before

But had killed each maiden on the wedding night

(for he was under a curse, you see)

I knew he had a past; so did I.

His past came knocking on my face

While mine got me called a slut.

When King Wivern was naked and shivering

His bride, still wearing a single shift,

Beat him with birch branches and bathed him in milk

Until he was a human prince,

Beautiful to behold

Was he on his best behavior for me?

Or I for him?

Did we change for each other,

And then revert to our worst?

At least I never raised a hand or voice.

While King Wivern was at war,

His wife was cast out

(by a jealous mother-in-law

who said she gave birth to puppies

and hid the real children)

Where did my husband go?

The man I loved and married?

Replaced by sullen stares,

Accusations,

It didn't matter what I said or did,

How often or how little we fucked.

Wandering in the forest,

The maiden met two enchanted princes:

A crane and a swan

Lonely, done, paperwork finished,

I wandered and wove in and out of crowds

Until I shaped a homecoming amidst

New friends that felt like old.

They were under a spell:

Doomed to remain in bird form

Until a woman who had given birth

Let them nurse from her

My hotel room.

I stripped for them, not caring

If I left on a single layer

To keep me apart, protected.

The maiden disenchanted them

By letting each bird suckle at her breast

And I, flushed with wine and flirtation

Bent both men to my breasts

And they sucked and sipped

Until I moaned and became

Something other than a discarded wife.

King Wivern returned from war

And wondered where his wife was

And went to find her

No more layers. No more compromises

Or complicated strip-teases to slip

Around saying what I actually want or need.

Only the magic of sweaty shared kisses.

King Wivern found his wife

Living with King Crane and King Swan

And proposed a test to see whom she preferred:

Lock her in a room without food or drink,

See whom she asked to toast her when they released her

One kisses me above and one below

("Save some for me," one says, with a wicked laugh)

And I writhe, and in this perfect moment

Begin to open and to heal.

She withstands the week and emerges

And asks King Wivern to drink to her

And returns home with him, but still loves King Crane

Who dies of a broken heart

One inside me and one without,

And we share and trade

And everyone is enamored, enchanted

And I am never going back

I will never be coerced again.

I have my two boys,

One at each breast,

This moment complete forever.

THE SLEEPER AWAKENED

You must remember that I smiled daily

through sleep-stained eyes,

accepted jewels from your hand,

each gem a weight on my neck,

a cruel pressure that stopped up my throat

and caged my voice

but nonetheless let it rest.

When one night of marriage flipped

into two, then three, then four,

it was as though the whole palace

seized and sighed, and servants

began to look me in the eye

and heed my requests.

My sister commanded an army of couriers:

sent them to the Maghreb, to the Mamluks,

to el-Andalus, to the Chola dynasty,

to warring Seljuqs and Jalayirids,

and oh the stories they brought back:

calligraphy on lamb-skin parchment,

papyrus, even paper from farther east.

Before, I had enough stories in me—

some from books, some from mouths—

to number as many as ants drawn to honey.

Within weeks, I had enough stories

to compete with the stars in the sky,

enough to keep me alive,

but still one was missing:

the story to buy my freedom.

An emissary from the clever Kabyles

laid one manuscript at my feet:

spooling threads of Maghrebi calligraphy

almost overflowing and spilling onto the rugs,

threatening to dye tassels with its rich blue ink

written in lilting Tifinagh script:

twenty tales, and one a key.

The peasant man switches places with a caliph

(my mind catalogues the motif,

coming up with 31 similar tales immediately)

who enjoys his loquacious inebriation

and dresses up the peasant in his clothes,

making him caliph for a day.

The peasant thinks himself caliph,

makes advances to the slave girls,

caresses them with words and callused hands

until one agrees to come to his bed:

but first, a meal, one she peppers with banj,

and the sleep that comes for him is swift,

his memories muddled.

Swallowed by sleep, the peasant

wakes in his own bed:

was he a caliph dreaming of being a peasant,

or a peasant dreaming of being caliph?

Two more nights the caliph tricks him;

two more nights the slave girl drugs him.

Eventually

the caliph reveals the ruse,

rewarding the peasant with wealth for life.

No more is written of the slave girl.

She disappears from the story.

The court chemist finds me banj,

laces it with poppy milk and other gifts

from loyal diplomats.

Loyal to me, I should specify.

I know how much you love your tea

before story-time. You've loved it for months now

...how many months? Ah. Good question, but

the main question now is:

Should you disappear?

Or should I?

THE WITCH'S HOUSE

"ok google, how do i cast a love spell"

So like there's this witch's house

"ok google, how do i know if my boyfriend is cheating on me"

I asked my sorority sister for directions
Because Google Maps can't find it
But it's near the nature trail where we used to run
And I think I can find it on my own.

"ok google, how do i know if my boyfriend is lying to me"

You have to go by the light of the full moon,

Sarah said, and put a childhood memory in one pocket

And a painful thing in the other (pictures don't count

And your phone's battery will die on the way no matter what

Even if you charged it beforehand, which I did,

But mine still died, in the middle of updating apps).

"ok google, what happens when you can't trust yourself anymore
but know you need help"

The witch's house is basically a Tiny House,

A cottage with an herb garden, while the witch

Is just a woman old enough to be my mom.

"ok google, what is gaslighting"

She asks for the memory, and I hand her the seashell

From that summer at the lake house with my family.

"ok google, what is emotional abuse"

She asks for the pain, and I hand her the necklace Mike gave me

On our one-year anniversary, two weeks before things got bad.

"ok google, how long does it take to recover from being abused"

Before she even asks the story spills out of me along with tears:

Suddenly we were fighting 24/7 and I didn't know why,

He didn't like me hanging out with my friends,

He was jealous of my study group which happened to be all guys,

He kept track of me by my Facebook activities

Even when we weren't supposed to hang out that day.

How I started to question if he loved me

And then the questions became what was even real anymore,

If my memories were accurate,

Which obviously didn't help my grades that semester.

(neither did the panic attacks)

She listened and listened and then she said

I can help you, I can cast a spell

To gather up the parts that are hurting

But I need you to know first that

You didn't ask for this, and you don't deserve it,

And I need your consent to proceed.

I'm still crying, basically choking on my tears,

I'm shaking under the weight of believing him,

Believing I was crazy for so long and now

I know it's not true, and I'll do anything to be me again.

He did not say this to you,

They never do,

But it was never about you,

It was about controlling you,

And it was wrong.

For a moment I'm scared that this will be worse

Than the pain I'm already in.

What I'll do is this:

Identify the places where his fingertips

Left impressions on your heart,

Begin to lift those indentations,

Smooth out their ridges.

It's tricky work.

There's risk, and there's a secret.

She reaches inside my ribs

And touches and tugs

—it hurts so bad I can barely breathe—

Oh child, you're better off without him.

He's the type who'd salt your skin out of spite

To keep your skeleton from donning it again

After a night of flying around, being your own woman.

—cries sear my throat,

I realize it's my own voice,

Erupting from me with all the anger

I never got to express—

This is the work, these are the words

—and I can breathe again—

The risk?

I might leave fingerprints of my own on your heart,

But they'll be there with your consent.

Come back if you crave organ meat more than usual,

And we'll talk.

—and I start to trust myself again,

Trust my decision to come here,

Trust that things will be okay.

The secret?

You can reshape them in time when you're ready.

Your heart is your own; it always has been.

Now you know what to guard against,

For others will always try to claim

Those they cannot control

Precisely because you're free.

"ok google, tell me some women's support groups on campus"

DOOR OF SWAN AND RAVEN FEATHERS

WOVEN OF SILENCE AND THISTLES

(OR, THE GIRLFRIEND'S STORY OVER MARTINIS)

It was like one of those stories

where the girl can't talk for seven years

or like the one where the Virgin Mary

sews her mouth shut. You know. Bad shit like that.

Right, so, in the story she has to keep quiet

because of a spell on her brothers who are swans

but for me the birds were all women, beautiful women,

the other women in his life. Alien avian women.

I accepted the curse. I knew I couldn't say anything bad

about them, since I knew about the whole thing,

we had the relationship talk and it was open

and it was cool since I'm really busy anyway, you know?

Things changed. Circles under his eyes and silence

between us, space between us in bed, all my words

pouring out to stone ears and I was ignored and nothing

I said mattered and I was silenced, silent, desperate.

The story's about suffering in isolation, right?

This girl weaving shirts out of nettles or thistles or

something unpleasant: well, there was burning all right.

A trip to the clinic. Medication to reduce future outbreaks.

There's no happily ever after or magic fucking pill

to fix this, to fix how I loved him and trusted him

and was fed my heart on a platter of thistles,

with a side of silence and, now, shame.

So fuck silence. I'm hunting for the flock of other women,

intimidating precisely because they're an unknown,

and I'm asking them: What was your story?

Who were you to him? Who are you now?

Which of you was a beast-bride, and which a red-cloaked girl,

which a necrophiliac's dream, which a pale queen?

Have you suffered silence, infection, and rage?

Or were you somehow treasured, exempt, lucky?

I'll listen. I'll buy the next round.

I'll help you break your curse, too.

THE TWELVE BROTHERS

The words of a girl who must mind twelve brothers
flow ceaselessly as a stream, skirting rocks and barriers,
leaping like frogs, with frogs, endlessly playing catch,
catch-up, chase this one, chastise that one.

The stepmother saw, and yes, she wanted the father's love
all for herself, to catch his eye every time, but also
she pitied the girl, saw a ghost of herself in the child
who sewed and sang and scrabbled to civilize.

A curse fell from the sky and scooped up the twelve boys,
stinging their skin with feathers new-grown,
molding lips into beaks, toes into talons,
while the girl watched helplessly.

"You can be quiet now," the stepmother said,

emerging from shadows, and the girl's sobs stopped up

her throat like a violently shaken bottle.

Reading her fear, the stepmother tried again:

"You can be quiet now, you needn't mind them

now that they've ravens. Keep silent for seven years,

and they will turn back into your brothers.

That time is your own."

Understanding now, the girl faded into the forest.

The ravens brought her morsels;

she wove clothes out of their feathers

to stay warm, to pass the time.

She rested, no longer bound to torrents of words,

endless exclamations, the tug on her heart

for every moment managed, each brother soothed.

The moment the enchantment expired,

the birds folded into boys, reverse origami,

bones lengthening and filling in with a gurgle,

feathers evaporating and skin shining through,

and still she did not speak.

This witch, that godmother, none could say why:

Was it another curse? A secondary enchantment triggered

by the release of the first? A potion, perhaps?

She eventually persuaded her brothers to stop inquiring.

Some of her brothers married; she played with the children,

a kind aunt to be pitied, taken in, never over-burdened.

Still she smiles, though only through closed lips.

SNOW WHITE GOES GRAY

For every silver hair I plucked

in my thirties, I am sorry;

now they spring up,

a reverse snowfall from

a bed of coal-black hair.

I am sorry too

about the red-hot iron shoes—

sorry that I accepted the corset stays,

the comb, the apple,

reveled in them, even;

sorry that I mistook

every sign from you as

hostility, not a warning.

Married to a prince anyway,

I miss my mother,

and I am sorry

we will not grow old together,

because you never showed me how.

SHELLS

You taught me to separate eggs,

your large hands cupping my small ones,

your wrinkled skin free of egg whites,

my fingers transparently coated.

When I was old enough to crack

eggs unaided, you ground ginger.

I rolled yellow suns in white skies,

yellow eyes in veined white sockets,

avoiding cracks as you taught me.

Mother, the jagged egg edges

never tore open a yolk

in your hands, unlike children's teeth,

white and biting, sharp and feral;

they snapped at you from the oven

like chicks pushed back into their shells.

Mother, you never taught me how

to live without you, what to do

alone in the gingerbread house.

I separate egg whites, alone now,

gently cracking each womb and tomb,

icy white and fiery yellow,

the white of bones untouched by hunger.

WALKING ON KNIVES

Being part of their world

will feel like walking on knives,

the sea witch said.

I agreed to it, to every condition,

so she cast the spell,

signed my degree,

and made the sea spit me up

like a bedraggled tea leaf.

The magic flowed around me:

nobody had heard of the university

where I did my PhD

but job offers bubbled up,

famous professors swam alongside me

like a school of fish at conferences.

I worked for it all—

each publication I hunted

as intently as a shark

and each course I designed

wily as an octopus solving a puzzle.

Better a professor than an ornamental princess,

even with the petty departmental politics.

Every day I wear heels to class

(because it all hurts the same)

and every night I email the sea witch

to meet our conditions:

she has Wi-Fi in that cavern of hers,

but she wants to devour this world's knowledge

before this world devours ours.

So it's PDF after PDF,

every institutional repository and database

that I can plunder, to feed her curiosity.

My sexy research agenda slows after a while,

growing mossy with age, a little too dated.

The university gives me first years.

I actually talk to my students

instead of singing spellbinding lectures

that leave them too awed to ask questions.

That's when I learn how cruel this world is,

how many of my students bear scars

on their insides, where I imagine

nascent pearls forming

as if they were oysters,

burnishing trauma with beauty.

Again and again, this world stabs and stabs at me:

not just my feet, but now my heart,

as I hear story after story from the lips of girls

ready to tip into adulthood.

The ocean does not lack for suffering,

but the humans choose to inflict it.

The research articles I send the sea witch these days

focus more on trauma, sexual assault, recovery.

The students who find me and stay with me

learn the secret names of sea urchins who unfurl

at a gentle touch, baring their soft bellies to stroke

and who will, if asked, release a spine tipped with poison.

The girls learn how to slip soundlessly in and out of the water,

which reefs are safe for humans and which are not.

When I am in the water with them my feet do not hurt,

but their wounds lap at my skin along with the waves.

Slowly I arm them with knowledge, with weapons.

Nobody cares what you do after tenure, anyway.

We take selfies while out hunting frat boys who hunt girls,

send them to the sea witch.

I eventually have to buy the sea witch a cell phone;

one of my girls wants to make her own deal

and this is the easiest way to arrange for them to talk

(I figure if the sea witch can shift my tail to legs,

remolding human genitals and nudging glands

to release the right hormones would be a lark).

The sea witch texts me constantly, always in caps.

KRISTY EXPLAINED WHAT DILATORS ARE,

DID YOU NEED ONE TOO?

CAN YOU COME SHOW ME HOW THE CAMERA
WORKS AGAIN?

WHY DIDN'T YOU TELL ME ABOUT SNAP CHAT???

After she threatens to show up

during one of my final exams

when I'd stopped responding to her texts,

I renegotiate our deal:

knowledge for knowledge still, yes,

but prearranged blackout times.

I don't ask her to take away the pain,

and she doesn't offer.

The knife-points prickle at my toes,

and the sea shines through when I smile.

It's enough.

Rapunzel's Mother(s)

No herb, no hunger.

No calories, no child.

The knots in my stomach began before the baby.

Anxiety pushed,

Depression pulled,

Snaking tendrils

Through my abdomen, clenching my mouth shut

And shaking my head with polite refusal:

No thank you, food doesn't sound good right now.

You tempted me with morsels—

Rib-eye to keep up my iron,

Kale chips to help with fiber—

And my stomach unclamped its hold

Long enough to let me be healthy enough

To conceive.

Eating for two should have been easy.

I curled into a ball around the pit in my stomach

But the nights passed slowly, sleeplessly.

You began to worry.

You introduced me to your dealer.

She'd been hooking you up

Long before you and I married.

She agreed to serve me without a green card

(because a pregnant woman smoking remains taboo

no matter what she's smoking).

It was under the table.

So we bartered.

She was lonely, no kids of her own,

She wanted to hang out with us more

Once we became a family.

You seemed cool with it at the time.

Getting slivers of sirloin

Past my lips was tough,

Especially with the morning sickness,

But she held my hair and helped

Me find my appetite again.

You drifted away, smoked between shots,

Chasing connection between whiskey bottles.

You sunk into yourself

As I found strength in her embrace

And flinched from your surly words.

You tried to take it all back,

Reclaim control over the source, the substance

That let me inhale nourishment.

I won't be displaced by my own damn dealer

You said, before deleting her from my phone,

Hiding the car keys,

Locking my world in isolation.

My doctors would've stayed clueless

But for the bruises: you only

Lost your temper once

But were careless enough to leave marks

On my arm (nowhere near my face or stomach,

You'd later protest in your defense)

When trying to grab me and hold me close

And prevent me from packing my things and going.

And now all I hear from you is

That bitch, that fucking witch

Who took me from you,

Who stole your child in exchange for some green.

Oh, no, you did that all yourself.

And now that I am leaving you,

The stomach-churning anxiety lessens daily

And I smoke less and eat more.

My friend and lover has a room in her apartment

And enough security to keep you out

While we make salads and knit baby blankets,

Preparing a lovely life for our child.

Rounded belly like a grapefruit,

I finally smile and release the weight of you

Buoyed by her healing hands

Running through my hair as she whispers,

You're safe, you're enough,

Never let anyone tell you otherwise.

You Can't Just Leave Your Car These Days

You can't just leave your car these days.

You need to drive it at least once a day,

maybe more, though it's worse in our town.

Just last week I heard the characteristic muffled

Sounds—bumps from under the hood,

rustling behind the dashboard—

but of course I couldn't get the rat out.

We have it better than Hamelin, though.

I was out driving

when I popped open the glove box.

A rat was staring out at me.

I screamed.

The kids screamed.

The rat screamed.

I slammed the glove box shut

and kept driving.

Both our towns reneged on our deals.

The Piper took Hamelin's children

after taking the rats.

We kept our kids,

but also kept the rats.

The rat must've eventually gotten bored

and left for a better home

(no chewed wires in its wake,

thank god).

My neighbors got a car-cat.

I might also, once the kids

are out of their car-seats.

Once the toys are cleaned out,

and the sippy cups,

and the binkies,

and the crumbs.

Some days I'm not sure

who got the better trade.

The Modern-Day Mermaid's Lament

The tales were right about one thing.

We are voracious.

Clad in white I lure lovers into my grasp;

No need to sing or stick to sailors.

I adapt to the times, cut my hair,

Enjoy your salty fleshy caresses without drowning

Very many of you, at least.

You humans

With your jargon, your need to put

Everything into tidy boxes—

I learned your words to chart my course,

Your poly and compersion and swingers.

I smile toothily as I utter them to strangers.

I lap up your desires

As one of your land mammals does fresh water:

Hungrily, greedily, knowing it sustains me

But not knowing why.

Our scholars were cataloguing types of intimacy,

Not anatomy. Back when we were enough.

You humans

Are our nourishment.

Bad enough you never believed in us;

Worse you never believed you could be

Symbiotic.

Like sea glass tumbled by the waves

I move under and over your bodies

(men, women, both, neither).

I love you all—that is what makes us monstrous to you.

Who among you could believe it, that love

Is so easily distributed without being diluted?

You humans

Could not love without owning,

Desire without possessing,

Enjoy without controlling.

There are too few of us now.

We have no support groups, no Wikis,

No Facebook groups or chat sites.

Your kind that are most like my kind

Are less marginalized now, less

Punished for your "open" relationships,

as though any relationship could be closed,

as though any ecosystem could be closed.

I pick my prey from your ranks,

Noting that lack of shame and secrecy

Flavors our interactions with a cleaner scent,

A mouthfeel reminiscent of the sea breeze

Back before industrialization.

You humans

Have discovered how to be like us too late.

Too late to save us, to preserve our species.

Perhaps not too late to save your own.

DOOR OF GOLD AND SILVER CROWNS

Blunt Weapon

They only call me when they desperately need me.

I am a blunt weapon.

If they call me godmother, witch, djinn—no matter.
They call, I answer.

I used to snarl defensively,

accused of clobbering fate,

being too unkind.

See? This child was virtuous, that one unworthy.

A second son in need of recognition,

a stepdaughter craving love.

Now I accept the insults and accusations.

They are all true.

I am too harsh.

I neglect many.

I pluck out eyes,

cut off hands,

Feed peasant girls

loaves of iron bread as they

search for their beloved.

Behind my mantle of thorns,

I know the truth:

I am harsh.

My methods are unorthodox.

But I play to my strengths,

leveling castles and crafting curses,

slicing off unneeded limbs to reveal

a body's true perfection,

an asymmetrical silhouette that will catch a king.

They only call me when they desperately need me.

I am a blunt weapon,

but not an unfair or unkind one.

I may wield the magic,

but their desires direct it.

This knowledge lets me sleep at night

(as my kind do, in our own fashion).

I cannot say the same for countless Cinderellas,

eyelids shuddering over dreamed memories

of sisters blinded and hobbled.

Was it worth it, pretty girl, helpless dreamer?

Trading your sisters for a prince?

I am the butcher knife your desire conjured;

You are the reason for my magic.

What a fine pair we'd make,

your hand pointing me in a direction,

leveling my wand like a sword

at any threat or braggart.

But of course I'm not cruel.

Your need summons and then dismisses me.

Plucking you out of your new life,

as easy as snatching an eye from its socket,

that would be the mean trick to play.

So I wait, and watch, until called upon again

(perhaps this time by a blind stepsister, or

by your daughter who will never live up to your beauty)

and I hone my magic, and dull my edges:

the better to bludgeon you with, my child.

DONKEYSKIN

I didn't always flinch at kindness
but now a stray hand at my elbow
to steady me while carrying trays
crumples me.

The first year after I left,
I was only good for washing dishes,
leaving my fur matted with water and lye
while my eyes stared unseeing.

There is no story to re-member:
here I am only a scared animal
that does as it is told
with quickly-working sooty fingers.

The second year after I left,

something inside me unfurled.

Whatever my father reached inside me and broke

stirred just a little.

Pastry blossomed under my fingers

transforming into sweet buttery shapes

with only a few stray hairs

and people noticed.

The third year after I left,

the cook stopped scolding me

the maids stopped teasing me

and if the prince noticed, I didn't.

I wove a beautiful thing

and only later knew it a net,

too absorbed by suds and sobs

that came on suddenly.

The fourth year I could breathe again,

wear the dresses without shuddering,

touch and be touched without freezing,

and I noticed the prince noticing me.

There is no story, but this is the truth:

a powerful king takes what he wants,

a mourning daughter yields,

a wise prince waits.

No godmother aided my flight.

I asked for the dresses on my own.

I did not escape unscathed.

But I did not let him attend my wedding.

It took five full years until I was ready

to drop my ring in the prince's cake batter

and reenter society on my own terms.

He's worth the wait; so, I learned, am I.

Mother of Swans

I lift this glass of wine

in your honor;

but to me, images form inside,

burgundy swirls clad in crystal,

and they speak.

Daughter, I tell you true:

your grandmother came from Pythia's line

and this is what I see for you:

twelve sons alight on wings of white

and a daughter made to mourn.

They leave you all,

and you cannot warn your girl

to beware of magic bargains,

beware of kings with kind eyes

and unkind mothers.

She cannot speak to say yes or no,

she cannot sing for joy

or cry for sorrow,

though thrice she will be tempted.

While your girl suffers

the others fly free,

and when she wins their freedom,

her hands stinging,

her soul condemned,

then she will think of you,

your body and heart torn

by birthing twelve boys

(and one girl),

and wonder if it was worth it.

Oh.

Hm.

Your guests, their faces...

What was I saying?

Let us drink to the health

of bride and groom.

Such a vision of love.

Daughter, visit me

someday.

You needn't

bear

all

this

alone.

TENACITY

Fairy tales taught me tenacity:

To seize life by the teeth

And tug until it broke

Or I did.

THE PRINCE'S SERVANT

my body as a tree is different

my legs, once strong, now roots

and my arms branches

and my hair leaves

my prince flies as a dove

a few hours every day

I let him scratch at my bark

even though as a man

he never touched me

he brings a maiden

he gives her a golden key

she enters me.

my insides, once kept separate

by skin, organs, muscles, tissue

now congeal into a room for the maiden

inside me a bed, a table with food,

and her.

and her.

my prince flies as a dove

(he never touched me as a man)

he brings the maiden

to the witch's house.

my insides, empty again.

(no heart to sorrow,

no tongue to plead)

she emerges with the golden ring:

breaking curse,

unmaking my tree-flesh,

disenchanting my prince.

my body, a man's again.

my body as a tree was different.

my prince flew as a dove.

he nested in me, but now nestles

the golden ring on the maiden's finger

she takes my prince in marriage

and I am once again empty.

Donkeyskin Does the Dishes

The air is cold, the water is hot:

the cold slaps my face, while the heat

grasps my hands, first a welcome embrace

then one growing rougher, raking claws

against finger and palm, reddening the whole

while I dream of the dress like the sun,

stored in a walnut shell under my bed,

a bed I can call my own even though it is small and humble,

a bed untouched by the stories of my mother's beauty, my father's madness,

and the sliver scrap of fabric sunbeam carries those memories,

is woven by their warped threads,

but the sun in my homeland shines warmer than the one here,

reminding me that if it can change, so can I,

and even with ravaged hands,

I have a piece of the sun

and with it, I will bloom when ready.

Fairies' Gifts

Fairies' gifts go beyond grace,

beauty, and charm;

I was the child gifted

justice, a yearning for fairness.

I prefer it to the other gifts

(who needs charm and grace anyway)

but I cannot befriend a cop,

I cannot pass up a protest,

I cannot look away from cruelty,

I cannot sleep unless

exhausted from straining for equity.

I know others have it worse,

but wow, my parents must have pissed off that fairy.

A Stinky Coat

We serve supper with a side of silence:

a mystery every dinner guest ponders

between courses, chewing questions

alongside sustenance.

We stop offering to take their coats

after one guest's mink stole

is ruined with brine,

and, oh, the smell.

We stop having guests at all.

The coat remains in the front closet:

a mystery, a secret, and finally, a truce.

No more dinner parties

where I show off my selkie wife,

her hung-up skin a silent testament

to how trustworthy I am,

to my connections to the land,

the indigenous votes I'll muster.

We'll get the backers some other way;

I'll become the first female candidate.

She squeezes my hand and sends me off

to another gala, staying home to eat sardines

and watch another nature documentary.

Snow White and Rose Red in Orlando

Giddy girls

holding hands

running here

running there!

We careen toward

cities of light—

but the lights recede,

forever out of reach

and your hand slips from mine....

I know you were just

guiding me through crowds,

giggling as we dodged

shambling tourist bodies.

I know we'll hold hands again,

pelt breathlessly through the hubbub,

I know it was just...

I know you were just...

And I just smile at you

a little more slowly

and sadly this time.

Excerpts from Hans Christian Andersen's "The Little Mermaid"

The little mermaid's sisters swam up to where she sat on the dock, and they presented her with a glittering knife. "If you kill the prince," they sang in forlorn voices, "you can return to us under the sea."

The sky is red, the sky turns orange, the sky weeps purple with grief. The little mermaid is stunned when she is finally allowed to swim to the surface to see the sky: such a giant block of one color, so different from the undulating watery views she grew up navigating. She knows this is temporary.

"But think again," said the witch, "for once you are human you can no longer be a mermaid: you will never return to your sisters or swim underwater; if you fail, you will become foam on the crest of the waves."

Her sisters try to tear the unconscious man from her arms. "Traitor!" they scream at her, for rescuing this human from the depths, but though she is the youngest she is the strongest of them all, and she beats at them with her tail while propelling the human up towards the surface.

The prince asked her who she was and where she came from, but she looked at him sorrowfully for she could not speak. At long last he brought her home to his palace, where beautiful female slaves, dressed in silk and gold, sang and danced. The little mermaid clapped her hands but carried sadness in her eyes: oh, if only she could sing sweetly once more.

He was kind to her. She would always remember that.

The oldest sister's birthday was in winter, so when she swam up to the surface for the first time, she saw large, beautiful icebergs. They glittered like diamonds and shone like pearls under the moonlight, and all the ships that came near veered away from the frightful storm that arose when the oldest mermaid hoisted herself onto an iceberg to watch the human-made objects cavort.

When the little mermaid goes ashore, there are no more icebergs.

She cast one more lingering glance at the prince, and then threw herself from the ship into the sea, and thought her body was dissolving into foam. The sun rose above the waves, and its warm rays fell on the cold form of the little mermaid, who did not feel as if she were dying.

She takes the knife her sisters gave her and uses the legs the sea witch granted her to find the king among men, the one she saved, and she catches him in a net of charming eyes and smiles. She waits until his meetings are over, until his slaves are gone, until his compound is all locked up.

She saw the bright sun, and all around her floated hundreds of transparent beautiful beings; she could see through them the white sails of the ship, and the red clouds in the sky; their speech was melodious, but too ethereal to be heard by mortal ears, as they were also unseen by mortal eyes.

The sky is red, the sky turns orange, the sky weeps purple with grief. The knife falls from her bloody fingers, and she hopes she is not too late, that the thrumming of her human heart is exhilaration, that the burning of her skin signals the flush of victory, and not the encroaching thirst of the sun that eradicates seasons, evaporates seas, igniting and ending the world.

Swan Maiden

travel-sized toothbrush

travel-sized makeup wipes

travel-sized affairs:

lightweight, single-use, no excess packaging

like the swan maiden herself, giddy-up girl,

feather up, webbed toes turn to talons,

fly away from another life.

Door of Bone and Ice Needles

SEASICK

Love makes me seasick

and I lurch along on land

as I walk home,

my heart limping behind me.

Home is a pit.

Home is a prison.

Every pot and knife a fishhook

embedding me deeper here.

Once I was free,

once I swam sleek.

But a bad man stole my skin

and the sea bled from my eyes.

I see through dry sockets

and I wash with chapped hands

trying to stem the unending tide

of kelpy rags and shell-white dishes.

Love is a net

but I am a clever fish;

I gnaw at the knots daily,

spurred by the sound of the chopping block.

Coat of a Thousand Furs

Animals are dumb

(I mean that in a good way, I promise).

I know because I was a princess.

My people gave me

Bangles & baubles

Until my mouth was stuffed up

With doubt and I could not speak:

Is this a true friend's gift,

A bribe, a torrent of flattery?

Consolation for my mother's death?

Something to blackmail me with

If it's later found in a man's bedchamber?

My father gave me dresses:

As gold as the sun,

As silver as the moon,

As sparkling as the stars.

Beauty to mask a monster's proposal.

You know the story.

My animals gave themselves,

No more, no less.

Wordless furry bodies pressed

Against me for comfort,

Gaping mouths asking for the same

Assurances of food, warmth, grooming.

By the time my father

Asked for my hand in marriage

My words had almost all fled,

Gone to ground,

Burrowed deep inside,

Hibernating.

I felt bad asking for the coat.

Physically bad—my voice had rusted

From lack of use, scraping out of my throat

As though my tongue had grown bristly,

In advance of the rest of me.

I kept my favorites alive, of course.

I asked for a coat of furs from the forest animals,

But still felt sick knowing what was coming,

My pets, my mute friends, my comfort.

Animals are dumb: their silence guaranteed.

The perfect conspirators.

Quiet lumps in my bed,

Like my corpse of a tongue

Immobile in my mouth.

Assemble enough small forest animals,

Household pets, more or less domesticated,

And you'll have enough blood

To make it look like a human bled out.

Add in a few pig bones,

Tear out tufts of your own hair,

Create a trail of bloody wolf prints

Leading away from the scene.

Of course I bled too.

They fought back, my only friends,

For what creature does not cling to life?

More than anything, though,

Animals are dumb because their faith is

A whole thing, not unbreakable

(We've all seen dogs mistreated,

Cats skittish around water because their

Kittens or littermates were drowned)

But rather, inviolable.

It's there or it's not,

The same way a forest is.

Now I am mute beast,

Escaped burly bride,

And I too shall be a dumb animal

Until my heart restores

And my tongue sheds its skin

And even then, I may keep this coat

Instead of shucking it

On the chance of a new human life.

I know all too well what humans are capable of.

The Path of Glass and the Path of Iron

Two paths are ours to walk,

Two lines cut through the hearts

Of all women:

The path of glass and the path of iron.

We all start on the path of marvelous slippers

And magic mirrors, beautiful gleaming reflections

Of who we are, who we should be, who we should

Fight bloody battles to remain.

The sparkle of a wedding ring, the tinkle

Of a wineglass: those sounds and sights

Structure our world.

No one can walk the path of glass forever:

It cuts up your feet

And you can see where the others lost their balance

Based on where the bloody foot prints

Teeter, spattering red droplets

That splash and splotch

And vanish.

They fall, perhaps to death,

Perhaps to the path of iron:

Iron shoes to wear out before we find our way again,

Iron loaves of bread to munch, to make us thin again,

Iron coffins to bury us in if we continue to stray.

Iron nails, iron pots and pans:

These things are dull and invisible like us,

The opaque reminder of how we used to shine.

Let us not speak of the path of the beast

Or the path of the blade,

Which our husbands and brothers

Must also navigate, no less treacherous.

Caught between these two paths

I wonder sometimes if there's a third,

If I might catch a ribbon of blood

Or a ray of moonlight

And ride it far away from here,

Unraveling the story that imprisons me

And all my lovers and siblings

(especially those ejected from their paths

for lack of conforming).

But for now I sharpen my smile

In the mirror's reflection

And put spikes in my ears

As if to say: *I am not your virgin bride*

Yet if you insist on treating me like one,

You will find no part of me soft or yielding,

No part of me meant solely for you,

Even if that dooms me to the path of iron.

A Letter Home

(AS DICTATED BY THE MAIDEN WHOSE HANDS WERE CHOPPED OFF)

I learned that love is a bridle:

yoking your needs to one another

and pulling as hard as you can

to not give too much ground.

I watched my mother act as your helpmeet

and knew that someday I too

would make a fine spouse

and take pride in hard work.

Of course we were poor.

Winters cut away

our stores,

our selves.

Father, you prayed for a miracle

and that man promised such wealth

in return for so little,

how could you not grant it?

I stood behind the apple tree,

I was the promised prize,

and your words unyoked me from our family

and gave my fate to that man.

If I stand in a circle of salt,

will it protect me from the man

only to let you in

with an ax?

The incremental slices of cold winter

did not prepare me

for the slice of the blade

you wield, father.

One stroke

released me

from your yoke

for good.

With the finality of an executioner

you severed my needs from yours:

we became un-kin, unbound,

and there was nothing to do but leave.

Just as your blade pushed you from me,

my tears repelled the man,

marking my path with

lonesomeness.

I fare well enough without my hands,

feeding myself by wit and mouth.

My heart is still in that circle of salt,

iced over, the price of your comfort.

Somewhere there is a man who'll wed me

and I'll wear his bridle, and he mine;

but while I wander, oh father,

I'll mourn the bright days at home.

And I'll wonder

which yoke inside you pushed or pulled

you to lift the ax, hurt me that bad,

sever us for good.

THE OLD KING DREAMS

The old king dreams:

the girl, *his* girl, giggling

as she disappears around a corner,

feet pattering, tail dragging behind her.

He runs after her, trying to catch a glimpse,

knowing what he will see:

the blond locks from his wife,

her sparkling eyes too,

but a face that is his, his, his.

And a lithe body draped in a skin,

the pelt of his favorite donkey,

the one he'd killed for her brideprice

(with every bray a gold piece would fall from its lips:

no more, but what was wealth without happiness?).

He turns the corner,

hoping to catch up and coddle his girl

and hold her tight and next—

But what rears up on hind legs is

no longer a human in an animal skin

or the size of a human, but larger,

and it sets upon him, ripping out

chunks of his flesh with knifelike hooves

and braying, blood-flecked teeth.

The old king screams until he wakes up.

He falls asleep again and dreams the same dream.

Bit gory, but it gets the job done,

says the fairy godmother,

after she and the girl visit the king's dreams.

The former princess nods.

You could undo it, you know, if you find a new home,

get betrothed, invite him, and cook him a meal

made entirely without salt.

Otherwise, he'll eventually die or go even madder

from lack of sleep, not sure which will happen first.

The girl shrugs, drawing the skin cloak around her

thin frame even tighter, clutching her bag

with dresses to secure her future.

I never really could cook, she says.

All right, replies the godmother.

Off we go then.

DADDY DEATH

Death is just.

Death is fair.

Death was ours first

and still he loves us best.

I only had one father that mattered:

Daddy Death, godfather to lost boys like me

who arrived alone and quaking, newborns at the gates

of the club, too new to know our language, our customs.

I was Daddy Death's favorite, strong and young,

a pup lapping up rules and adoration and learning so quickly

to spot our kind in the waking world:

the closeted businessman, father of four;

the baker, the lawyer, the burly school bus driver;

and more politicians than I could count.

I eyed them all, a specter of Daddy Death in my vision

nodding, as if to say, *he is one of ours,*

he belongs to our underworld,

if only he'd let himself.

Daddy Death is fair and even-handed with all

(even me; especially me)

bears and pups and dykes and more

meting out punishment when deserved

but oh so tender, so gentle with aftercare.

That was before the rumors,

the slow illness preying on us;

whispering *grid, gay, go away*

and the clubs closed as the body count rose.

Aging monarch on shadowy throne:

Daddy Death lasted longest

but stopped going out

(except for the appointments)

and I was his messenger boy.

I, who passed well enough in the straight world;

I, who charmed all the pharmacists;

I, who could still see unerringly

when I meet a man:

he is one of ours; he may yet escape the plague

though Daddy Death looms over his bed

each night, an invitation, a warning,

a man whose heart can hold us all.

Love is a door, love is a dungeon

where a tender man presses pain

into your skin and shows you to yourself.

Daddy Death waits for me in the next world

while I do his work in this one, shepherding boys

so young to be in so much pain, but so was I at that age,

and now we know so much more,

and the medicine takes root in our bodies,

and though decimated, we grow strong again.

EVIL EYE

There's a Norwegian legend about a girl who's a witch:

She gives the evil eye to a neighbor's cow,

Killing it instantly.

The priest identifies her by talking to her

And she is killed.

She should have known:

Don't trust men.

There's a Palestinian folktale about a woman

Who marries a rich man and

Who lets in an old neighbor woman

With a wedding gift:

A blue bead to avert the evil eye.

The old woman is a ghoul,

The bead magically opens the door at night,

And the ghoul eats up the woman.

She should have known:

Don't trust women.

There's an Indian folk belief about a young mother

Who dresses her baby boy as a girl

To misdirect the evil eye.

Because who would want to curse a girl?

Who wants a girl in the first place?

(her husband being rich enough

to pay the bribes

for an illegal sex determination test,

followed by an illegal abortion,

for how many girls before that?)

She should have known:

Don't trust your desires.

Don't be a woman who attracts the attention of others

Don't be a woman who attracts attention

Don't be a woman who attracts

Don't be a woman

Don't be

Don't.

TRAFFICKED

Trafficked for a salad spinner's

worth of greens, "rescued"

for a life of being redeemed—

—never on my own terms,

never able to write my own ending—

When a girl says yes

to the first guy she meets

when a girl gets pregnant

when a girl doesn't conform:

it's always daddy issues,

never disenchantment

with the capitalist magic castle

that says use your body this way,

not that; marriage is a haven,

never exploitation, unlike

what *those* girls do with their bodies

—let down your hair,

it looks prettier that way—

Praise your rescuers,

write your memoir,

how could anyone consent

to being used like that,

clearly a girl could not

say yes to a life like that

but now you're all better

—more feminine—

BLUEBEARD

Maybe

Bluebeard

wanted

his

wife

to

be

a

monster

just like him

to open the forbidden door

see the corpses

close the door

return the key

and secretly revel

in having

a fearsome spouse

to

match

her

own

soul.

AFTERWORD

Here, I put some of my poetry into context, both in terms of the fairy-tale genre as a whole, and in terms of my personal life, and I hope that my tone is more accessible than most of my academic writing while still managing to convey some creative and/or intellectual insights. Mostly, I want the poems to stand by themselves and evoke whatever feelings, images, and associations they do for their readers...but because I'm also an academic who writes scholarship on fairy-tale poetry, and I love to nerd out about this stuff, I thought I would include an afterword that discusses some of my poetry in terms of influences and inspiration, since I view myself as participating in a centuries-long tradition of telling and retelling fairy tales through language and art. If this is your jam too, please read on; if it's not your thing, no worries.

The way scholars have tended to think about fairy tales for a while now is that they're poetic but that doesn't necessarily make them poetry. However, there are striking similarities between fairy tales and poems: both condense human experience into sharp, stark imagery, and both utilize an economy of words to convey a depth of emotion and experience (well, except for those long, twisty fairy tales penned by French women in the 1690s; but their flowery excesses are also reminiscent of some poetry from certain time periods). Many poetic traditions have structures and formulas, as do fairy tales; once you know what you're looking at in terms of fairy-tale plot structures, it's much like understanding the construction of a sonnet or a villanelle.

Both genres also leave much to interpretation. Despite the modern tendency to say "the moral of the story is..." many fairy tales are amoral, or have more than one moral, or have a crappy moral (I see "might makes right" in the punitive endings of many of the Grimms' tales, and surely that can't be right). Instead, I prefer to think of fairy tales as having potential messages, and how we decode these messages depends on our social positions as much as the identity and intentions of the author, which only gets more complicated when we consider that many fairy tales don't have original authors, but rather have been passed along by oral tradition (occasionally popping in and out of print) for centuries. While many fairy tales have acknowledged authors, some do not, and plenty of tales respond to other tales, and all of this is true of poetry as well, leaving us with a complex web of potential meanings to detangle in both genres.

Further, there's been a lot of scholarship on the language and style of fairy tales that hints at their kinship with poetry: their use of opening and closing formulas like "once upon a time," their limited color palette that emphasizes metals and the red/white/black trinity, the repetition of things occurring in threes, and so on. Max Lüthi's book *The European Folktale: Form and Nature* analyzes many of these stylistic traits of fairy tales. Some fairy tales contain poetic phrases (which translation into a new language can of course disrupt), such as the famous line from "Snow White": "Mirror, mirror, on the wall, who's the fairest of them all?" Most fairy tales, however, are entirely in prose, or story narration using a combination of dialogue, action, and so on, to convey what happens in the story. Still, many authors are drawn to the congruence between the two genres.

In the U.S., fairy-tale poetry took off in the 1970s, with some stellar feminist works like *Transformations* by Anne Sexton and *Beginning with O* by Olga Broumas. Many of these are raw pieces that question the fairy-tale happily ever after, focusing on the voices of female characters who explore their abuse and trauma within the tales. I think I first found some of these works during my folklore coursework in college and grad school, and they really resonated with me, since I also prioritize gender in my work on fairy tales.

Many poets followed suit in the 1980s and 1990s, with authors such as Jane Yolen, Margaret Atwood, Ellen Kushner, Delia Sherman, and Holly Black among others penning fairy-tale poetry alongside their prose works. Terri Windling's website Endicott Studio hosts a fantastic collection of fairy-tale poems by these authors and more, while Wolfgang Mieder's book *Disenchantments: An Anthology of Modern Fairy Tale Poetry* offers yet more poems.

When I started writing and sharing my fairy-tale poetry, inspired by many of the poems and authors listed above, I wanted to use poetry to explore my feelings and experiences. Since fairy tales often feature depthless characters (people without a lot of backstory or motivation), they're perfect for stepping into or projecting onto, plus I liked the idea of juxtaposing fairy-tale styles, structures, and characters with modern-day life. And as I am a somewhat private person despite latching onto internet spaces for sharing and community early on (anyone remember Livejournal?), I liked the idea of using fairy-tale language to obliquely express things I have felt without revealing too many details. I also have to inhabit a fairly serious academic persona for many of my waking hours, so it's fun to have playful and even cheeky moments in my writing, which I feel are not available to me on a regular basis. Unfortunately, it's something many academics coming from historically marginalized backgrounds face: if we don't act like serious scholars 24/7, it's all too easy for people to dismiss the significance of our scholarly contributions, our teaching, and so on.

However, I should note that not every poem in this collection is autobiographical; I have a strong preference for a first-person confessional tone, but it does not mean that I myself am the narrator (which is something I would really like readers to keep in mind, especially if you know me in real life...just because my characters get up to all kinds of adventures doesn't mean I have done the same!). But because, as noted, many classic fairy-tale characters lack interiority, I like to breathe some of my own experiences and emotions into them, to see if I can take away some of their flatness and infuse them with things similar to or parallel to my own life.

In fact, I actively discourage readers from looking for correspondences between my poetry and my life. It honestly feels weird and invasive to me for someone to do this...or at least tell me you're doing it, so err maybe don't loop me in on those conversations. This could be because I survived emotional abuse (particularly gaslighting) within the last decade (see my poem "The Witch's House" for an account of how that felt), and thus it would feel extremely icky for someone to assert that they know me in some intimate capacity when we don't actually know each other that well, or to speak in ways hinting that they know more about me than I do. You can count on some things in my poetry being true about me (I'm a feminist; I'm queer), but not every single thing mentioned in my poems is also reflective of my life experience. For example, in "Woven of Silence and Thistles," my narrator is in an open relationship that sours, and she realizes that though her partner (soon to be ex-partner) didn't technically cheat on her, he obscured some things, and that's why she took a trip to the clinic and was likely diagnosed with an STI (sexually transmitted infection). While I believe in regularly getting tested for STIs if one is sexually active, that's not a one-to-one recap of my life experience.

Rather than discussing every single poem, I'll highlight a few here. I have a particular fascination with ATU 510B, "The Dress of Gold, of Silver, and of Stars" (and if you don't know what ATU/tale type numbers are, basically, folklorists have long assigned numbers to distinct fairy tale plots to make them easier to track across space and time, in part because their titles are always changing when they're told in different languages; I go into more detail on this reference system in my book *Fairy Tales 101* in case you're curious). I've written numerous academic papers on this Cinderella variant, which has the fancy outfits and balls, but swaps in an incestuous father for the villainous stepmother as the source of the heroine's troubles. Thus, it should not come as a surprise that I've written numerous poems exploring this tale type: "Donkeyskin" is about healing, "The Old King Dreams" is about revenge, and "Coat of a Thousand Furs" is about survival at any cost. And recently I wrote "Donkeyskin Does the Dishes," which is both about hope and healing as well as about chronic hand pain, which I also experience.

While we don't have an annual fairy-tale conference, fairy tale scholars tend to carve out our own niches in existing conferences. You can usually find some of us at conferences devoted to folklore, literature, pop culture, and so on. So when a fairy-tale-specific conference is planned, you can bet many of us are all in. One of those times was in 2017, when a conference titled Thinking with Stories was planned in Detroit. It was mostly an academic conference, but there were some creative workshops too, and I remember that my colleague Veronica Schanoes led a session on retelling fairy tales. In one part of it, we were encouraged to juxtapose a fairy tale with a specific historical time period and see what happened. I'll admit that for a while I had nothing coming to mind. But then I got the idea to write a version of "The

Twelve Dancing Princesses" set in the U.S. right after World War II, with a woman who was technically married, but kept going out dancing with her lady-friends, finding that she preferred their company to those of men, but she didn't get a happily ever after; instead, she was caught and basically institutionalized for the crime of being queer. I don't view this as a big divergence from many versions of the tale, in which the princesses' nightly treks are halted by whatever masculine savior figure is the main character who then marries one of the princesses, and I often wonder for whom the tale's happily ever after is actually, like, happy. That poem is "What happened to the 12th dancing princess (circa 1946)."

"Daddy Death" came out of my fury at how the U.S. government handled the HIV/AIDS epidemic, my desire to write a "Godfather Death" retelling, and my idea to combine these two things by giving Godfather Death's godson the ability not to heal people, as in the tale text, but rather some sort of supernatural gaydar. I also tried to pay homage to the gay leather scene, to which I am an outsider, but a sympathetic one, as I am also a queer-flavored human.

I didn't think I had a retelling of "The Little Mermaid" in me since it's been done (and done well) by plenty of other people before...but then I came up with two. "Walking on Knives" has the mermaid come above land to become a professor (why else?!) after she strikes a bargain with the sea witch to feed her knowledge even though the sea witch remains under the sea: "she wants to devour this world's knowledge/before this world devours ours." Eventually the mermaid earns tenure, gets bored, and starts actually talking to her first-years, then learns just how much abuse teenage girls put up with. She then puts one of her students, a trans woman, in touch with the sea witch: "I figure if the sea witch can shift my tail to legs/remolding human genitals and nudging glands/to release the right hormones would be a lark."

I don't view myself as someone who does a lot of ecological activism, despite the fact that I grew up in a family that prioritized being ecofriendly whenever possible, and I would say it's a value I hold today. So, I was surprised to realize that the environmental hints of the previous poem, like the sea witch urgently wanting to learn about the above world before it devours her world, were set to appear in another of my pieces. This one is more of a prose-poem hybrid but I think of it as poetry, so I'm calling it such. It has an unwieldy title ("Excerpts from Hans Christian Andersen's 'The Little Mermaid'"), but that's because I wanted to use the title to suggest that I was juxtaposing phrases from Hans Christian Andersen's original tale with something else. That something else turned out to be a sorta post-apocalyptic version of "The Little Mermaid" wherein the mermaid goes to dry land in order to kill a despot before he can wreck the environment any more.

"You Can't Just Leave Your Car These Days" is based on a family story. My dad's car kept getting invaded by rats who were chewing on other wires and getting up to other mischief (apparently this is not uncommon, depending on the make and model of your car). One time my dad opened his glove box, saw a rat, and promptly closed it. There may have been some screaming involved. When I heard this story, I knew I needed to make it the central image of a retelling of "The Pied Piper" in some fashion.

I came up with the premise of "The Twelve Brothers" during the spring semester of 2021. The COVID-19 pandemic had been going on for around a year; I'd been let go from my teaching job in spring 2020, then asked back for fall 2020, basically so I could teach in-person classes that tenured professors had noped out of for health and safety reasons. This did not lead to a lot of good feelings on my part, but hey, at least I had health insurance again. The problem, though, was that I was teaching classes that had to be hybrid so the classrooms would be at half-capacity to lessen our chances of contracting COVID-19. So I had half my students come one day of the week and the rest Zoom in, and it switched every other day. I was exhausted from teaching in this new modality, I was sick of talking to my laptop camera, and I was sick of talking in general. Since I was also teaching about fairy tales then, I began wondering if there was a way to reframe silence as a good thing, since it's usually the result of a curse in fairy tales...and that's when I had the idea to retell ATU 451, "The Maiden Who Seeks Her Brothers," from the angle of the heroine actually enjoying not being able to talk. Sometimes silence can be a balm and blessing, rather than a disempowering curse. I wrote another ATU 451 retelling in a Storied Imaginarium workshop with Carina Bissett, "Mother of Swans," this one from the perspective of the mother of the woman who will give birth to the boys who will become enchanted, with a bit of an oracle/prophecy connection woven in.

I also noticed while putting together this collection that I've published multiple scholarly essays on ATU 451 and I have written multiple poems on it; similarly, ATU 510B has occupied a lot of my scholarly time (I argued about it with Alan Dundes in undergrad, and after he encouraged me to do my own research on the tale, it became my master's thesis and a subsequent publication), and I have written multiple poems on that tale type as well. So it seems that Vanessa Joosen's assertion that creative and scholarly interpretations of fairy tales feed one another in her book *Critical and Creative Perspectives on Fairy Tales: An Intertextual Dialogue Between Fairy-Tale Scholarship* applies to individuals as well as to broader time periods and intellectual movements.

I played a little fast and loose with some dates in "The Sleeper Awakened," which is based on both the frame tale of *The Thousand and One Nights* and a tale within it, "The Sleeper and the Waker," ATU 1531, "Lord for a Day," which is also found in Shakespeare's *Taming of the Shrew*. Informed readers will know that the earliest full text of the *Nights* dates back to a 15th century Syrian source (in Arabic, as were most manuscripts until Antoine Galland's translation into French in the early 1700s, which also introduced new tales like "Aladdin" into the text), and that we have records of this collection existing from the 9th century onward. I placed Scheherazade (and her sister, who plays a role in many older texts as well) in the 13th or 14th century, which is probably too late given the historical records...plus, this being a folktale, she probably never existed in the first place. But I like the idea of Scheherazade commanding an army of spies and scribes to keep her supplied with tales, and also the idea that she wins in the end, not by healing the king's misogynistic murderous madness with storytelling and love, but that she got ahead with wiles and never lost sight of the fact that she'd been married to a killer. I also give a rather large nod to the Amazigh people of North Africa for being the originators of the tale that saves her, which is a strange bit of serendipity since further research reveals that one of the oldest dated "dreaming man" variant of this tale comes from a 13th century Tunisian manuscript titled *A Hundred and One Nights*, Tunisia being part of the Maghreb, or Amazigh North Africa, which I had referenced in the poem before knowing any of this. Acclaimed *Nights* scholar Paulo Lemos Horta has an excellent article on this topic if you wish to know more.

While digging through some old emails I came up with a poem I'd written in 2012, submitted somewhere (it was rejected) and apparently completely forgotten about, "The Prince's Servant." It's based on a somewhat obscure fairy tale that I encountered in the Grimms' tale, "The Old Woman in the Woods" (ATU 442) where a servant girl is beset by robbers and then lost in the woods, and then a dove brings her a key that unlocks a tree so she can go inside and rest and eat stuff there. Then the dove has her enter a witch's house to retrieve a ring, which turns out to disenchant the prince (who has been turned into a dove) as well as all his servants, who have been turned into all the nearby trees. So of course I started thinking about how weird it would be to be a human turned into a tree and then to have a human enter your trunk which is also now magically a room...and of course I had to queer it up some.

These are some of the poems I can most clearly explain in terms of their origins and inspirations. The rest are either quite fuzzy, or they feel more private to me, so I prefer to let readers make of them what they will.

This book's organization came about while I was at a conference in 2023, Norm and Transgression in the Fairy-Tale Tradition. I'd had the idea for my collection, but wanted to organize it somehow, rather than just dumping 40ish poems on the reader all at once. My colleague Christy Williams had the idea of sorting the poems thematically in terms of doors and keys, which got me thinking about what fairy-tale doors might lead to, or from: love, sorrow, and other sorts of emotions and experiences, which I thought to concretize in terms of being rose doors or bone doors, thorn doors or ice doors. That ended up being rather unwieldy, especially since I was also trying to think of a title, so after the 2024 annual meeting of the American Folklore Society I asked some of my fairy-tale colleagues for input in a group chat we'd created, and Claudia Schwabe put me onto the kernel of what would become the current title. Thanks also go to Linda Lee, Abby Heiniger, and Kristi Willsey for weighing in on the title, and for my editor Susan Redington Bobby for making suggestions on the subtitle.

I think that's all I have to say about the roots and connections of this book of fairy-tale poetry. I'll end it with one of my favorite closing formulas (the last lines in a fairy tale after the story has wrapped up), from the Jack Zipes translation of Laura Gonzenbach's Sicilian fairy tales in *The Beautiful Angiola*: "The king and

Maruzza lived for a long time still, rich and consoled, and we have nothing as we get old."

If you enjoyed *The Thorn Key*, check out *Fairy Tales 101*, my approachable introduction to the study of fairy tales: their history, major concepts and themes, and a guide to the most important collectors and writers from the past few centuries through the present-day boom in fairy-tale retellings.

If you want to learn more about folklore in general, check out *Folklore 101*, my first book and a massive tour of the field of folklore studies. With a guide to significant concepts like tradition and folk group and chapters on the most important global folklore genres (from myths to jokes, and urban legends to rituals), this book offers a complete introduction to what folklore is and why it's relevant.

Appendix of Tale Type Numbers

In fairy-tale studies, we utilize established numbers to refer to the plots of internationally distributed folktales and fairy tales, since their titles often change as the tales are translated and told in different languages. The proper convention is to write "ATU (whatever number)," and readers will understand that we're referring to the Aarne–Thompson–Uther number assigned to that tale (for a more complete history of the tale type index, please see my book *Fairy Tales 101*).

All tale type numbers refer to the most current edition of the tale type system as of the time of publication. For reference, please see Uther, Hans-Jörg, et al. *The Types of International Folktales : A Classification and Bibliography, Based on the System of Antti Aarne and Stith Thompson*. Suomalainen Tiedeakatemia, Academia Scientiarum Fennica, 2004. 3 volumes.

302 The Ogre's (Devil's) Heart in the Egg: "Ogre Heart," "Secrets"

306 The Danced-out Shoes: "What Happened to the 12th Dancing Princess"

310 The Maiden in the Tower: "Rapunzel's Mother(s)," "Trafficked"

312 Maiden-Killer/Bluebeard: "Bluebeard"

327A Hansel and Gretel: "Shells"

332 Godfather Death: "Daddy Death"

425C Beauty and the Beast: "Beauty & the Beast in Berkeley," "Given or Sold or Stolen Away"

426 The Two Girls, the Bear, and the Dwarf: "Snow White & Rose Red in Orlando"

433B King Lindorm: "Given or Sold or Stolen Away," "King Wivern"

441 Hans My Hedgehog: "Hedgehog"

422 The Old Woman in the Woods: "The Prince's Servant"

451 The Maiden Who Seeks Her Brothers: "Mother of Swans," "The Twelve Brothers," "Woven of Silence and Thistles"

510A Cinderella: "Blunt Weapon"

510B Peau d'Âne/The Dress of Gold, of Silver, and of Stars: "The Coat of a Thousand Furs," "Donkeyskin," "Donkeyskin Does the Dishes," "The Old King Dreams"

570* The Rat-Catcher/The Pied Piper of Hamelin: "You Can't Just Leave Your Car These Days"

706 The Maiden Without Hands: "A Letter Home"

709 Snow White: "Snow White Goes Gray"

710 Our Lady's Child: "Woven of Silence and Thistles"

898 Daughter of the Sun: "Betrothed to a King"

1531 Lord for a Day: "The Sleeper Awakened"

ACKNOWLEDGEMENTS

I've always had the sense that I'm just a strange little nerd doing my thing and somehow I've lucked into being surrounded by loving, supportive people who cheer me on. The first accolades, as always, must go to my family: my mother and father and sister, but also my aunts and my grandparents (who have always politely asked to see my poetry, even when it's on intensely personal or bizarre topics).

Thanks go to my editor Susan Redington Bobby, who has also been a colleague in fairy-tale studies (before we even started working together on these publishing endeavors, I wrote a book review of one of her edited essay collections, and that put us on each other's radar), and to my cover designer Cover Villain, who has once again knocked it out of the park.

The editors who've seen something worth publishing in my work have been amazing to work with; special thanks go to Rose Lemberg and Shweta Narayan of *Stone Telling* for accepting my very first fairy-tale poem that was ever published, "Woven of Silence and Thistles." A.J. Odasso and Romie Stott at *Strange Horizons* have also been incredibly kind.

I've mentioned a number of my fairy-tale colleagues in the afterword, but basically they're all awesome and it's a delight to be able to work alongside such wonderful humans. I only wish we got to see each other more often than the conference circuit allows.

My friend Aradia read some of the more recent poems soon after I'd written them. My sister Sam has read a ton of my poetry. My friend and colleague Carina Bissett has also seen some of these more recent poems and created community for us fairy-tale writers. Friends and colleagues Sara Cleto and Brittany Warman deserve all the accolades and sparkles for encouraging creativity in fairy-tale realms.

To all those who've come and gone from my life, for better or for worse (but mostly for worse)...at least I got some poetry out of it. And better boundaries.

ABOUT THE AUTHOR

Jeana Jorgensen earned her PhD in folklore from Indiana University. She researches gender and sexuality in fairy tales and fairy-tale retellings, folk narrative more generally, body art, dance, sex education, disability, and feminist/queer theory. While she spends most of her time teaching college courses at Butler University and publishing her research, she also writes fiction and poetry. Her poetry has appeared in *Strange Horizons*, *Liminality*, *The Orange & Bee*, and *Glittership*, among other publications. She is a member of the Science Fiction and Fantasy Poetry Association and a member of the editorial team of *Marvels & Tales: Journal of Fairy-Tale Studies*. Her poem "The Witch's House" was nominated for the 2018 Rhysling Award, and her short dystopian story about reproductive rights, "The book you find when you really can't afford to get pregnant," won the Spider Road Press Feminist Flash Fiction Award of 2018. She also teaches dance, nurtures her sourdough starter, and knits. You can join her newsletter to keep up with her exploits at folklore101.com.

www.ingramcontent.com/pod-product-compliance
Lightning Source LLC
Chambersburg PA
CBHW021155130626
46554CB00005B/1835